IMAGES
of America

CATHOLIC
NEW HAMPSHIRE

Manchester, N. H. St. Joseph's Cathedral.

Located on the corner of Pine and Lowell Streets, St. Joseph Cathedral's brick exterior symbolized strength and stability to its mostly immigrant congregation. Emerging from the dark years when Catholics could not build churches in the center of cities, its steeple was visible from every downtown view. Its bells proclaimed the sacramental presence of Catholics throughout the city. (Courtesy of the Ken Francher collection.)

ON THE COVER: Rev. Edward A. Clark, vested in a cope, and officiating priests in Roman-Gothic lace alb and chasuble, known as a fiddleback, are receiving a deacon clothed in a traditional dalmatic in St. Joseph Cathedral. Holy Mass is celebrated at the marble reredos. Sacred art to the left of the altar portrays the nativity and to the right of the altar the Holy Family. The oakwood Communion rail with a bronze gate distinguishing the nave from the sanctuary has been removed. (Courtesy of the Manchester Diocesan Archives.)

For Joanne

IMAGES
of America

CATHOLIC
NEW HAMPSHIRE

For the love of our faith
Barbara D. Miles
October 12, 2021

Barbara D. Miles
Introduction by Msgr. Anthony R. Frontiero

ARCADIA
PUBLISHING

Published by Arcadia Publishing
Charleston, South Carolina

Printed in the United States of America

Library of Congress Control Number: 2019957035

For all general information, please contact Arcadia Publishing:
Telephone 843-853-2070
Fax 843-853-0044
E-mail sales@arcadiapublishing.com
For customer service and orders:
Toll-Free 1-888-313-2665

Visit us on the Internet at www.arcadiapublishing.com

This work is dedicated to Bishop Denis Mary Bradley, who lit the candle of faith that we, please God, keep aflame.

CONTENTS

Gradually, cities throughout the diocese were populated by Catholics, Christians, and Jews who cultivated old country values associated with education, religion, the arts, industry, leisure, and economic stability. Parochial and public schools rose on city blocks, newspapers and local publications kept the public informed, opera houses and theaters provided unique talent, and immigrant families adopted to the bustle of 19th-century American metropolises. Introduction of the railroad enabled greater mobility and expanded business and trade opportunities beyond the ferry and steamboat era.

Just as Catholics populated urban areas for employment in mills, so too did they plow the land, till the soil, and breed cattle, horses, pigs, sheep, and chickens as measurable accomplishments in farming. Catholics forged their way through forest thickets to harvest timber needed to build homes, public offices, and churches. In the disappearing years of the 19th century, most of the indigenous people of New Hampshire had either perished or were driven from their lands. Their absence resulted in prospects for rural life to those who would develop their camps, harvest their forests, fish and hunt their waters and woods, and plant produce to keep the next generation of families alive.

Southern regions of the diocese prospered more rapidly than their neighbors to the north. With a slightly more temperate climate and modestly extended planting, reaping, hunting, and fishing seasons, Catholic business leaders and homemakers suffered less hardships than those communicants in northern missions.

Orator Thomas Starr King describes highlands inhabitants as follows: "Those who need the patience of the mountains, that after thunder and hail and violent storms, peek out to sunshine with no bravado, as though on their mission to suffer and be strong."

While studying lichens and other alpine plants in the North Country between 1840 and 1850, Protestant botanist Dr. Edward Tuckerman described awe-inspiring scenery with a quote from the Old Testament *psalmoi* "songs sung to a harp." Psalm 50:2 states, "Out of the perfection of beauty, God hath shined." Contrast these observations with those of Catholic missionary Rev. Isidore H. Noiseux, assigned to all the territory in the Connecticut Valley up through the White Mountains. "Catholics living in the Upper North Country are often too poor to own a cow, the tones of their voices are saturated with misfortune. They are paid $1 a day lumbering the deep forests, living in cottages with walls not tight enough to keep out rain and snow." Mindful of the preceding and proceeding years of Catholic presence in New Hampshire, this pictorial journey begins in 1848 with the arrival of Rev. William McDonald, the first resident priest in Manchester. With a few excursions into the 21st century, the publication concludes with portraits of retired and deceased lay and episcopal leaders whose light continues to shine in our midst. As best as possible, *Catholic New Hampshire* traces 130 years of humble beginnings, significant accomplishments, and the extraordinary lives of ordinary men and women following the footprints of our faith through the grace of God, his only begotten Son, Jesus Christ, and our Advocate, the Holy Spirit, who remains ever with us.

—Msgr. Anthony R. Frontiero, STD
Incardinated priest of the Diocese of Manchester
and rector emeritus of the St. Joseph Cathedral

One

A BRIEF HISTORY OF THE DIOCESE OF MANCHESTER
HAYFIELDS TO HILLTOPS

The first heraldic shield of the Diocese of Manchester features the mitre of Bishop John Carroll, placed atop the coat of arms. A silver tincture, or metal background, presents a cross of gules. Five arrows representing the original counties of New Hampshire are securely fixed in a sheath, symbolizing unity. Coursing through the arrows, a staff's triumphant lily honors St. Joseph, patron of the diocese. (Courtesy of the Manchester Diocesan Archives.)

As descendants of the Premier See of Baltimore, established in 1789, New Hampshire came under the jurisdiction of the Archdiocese of Boston until 1855, when Blessed Pope Pius IX created the Diocese of Portland. He appointed the Right Reverend David W. Bacon bishop of Maine and New Hampshire. For 20 years, Bishop David Bacon extended his shepherd's hand across the vast wilderness of the two states. (Courtesy of the Portland Diocesan Archives.)

In 1875, the Right Reverend James Augustine Healy became the second bishop of the Diocese of Portland, which included the state of New Hampshire. For the following nine years, Bishop Healy and his chancellor, Rev. Denis Bradley, traveled by canoe, carriage, horseback, and train throughout the vastly rural northern New England states ministering to the few and far between faithful. They established missions and parishes and recruited priests, sisters, and laypeople to teach Catholics how to be Catholic. Mindful of the ethnic immigrant diversity, Bishop Healy founded 11 missions and parishes for the French, Irish, and English-speaking Catholics in rural, urban, and remote locations. (Courtesy of the Portland Diocesan Archives.)

POPE LEO XIII

With the pontifical authority of Pope Leo XIII, the state of New Hampshire became the Roman Catholic Diocese of Manchester, with the largest populated city designated as its episcopal seat. Two months after receiving the papal decree, Rev. Denis Mary Bradley was consecrated the first bishop of Manchester on June 11, 1884. (Courtesy of the Boston Archdiocesan Archives.)

On March 3, 1813, Eliza was born into slavery in Jones County, Georgia. Michael Healy bought 16-year-old Eliza for $600. She gave birth to 10 children, nine of whom survived to adulthood. Michael Healy moved their children to the North to be educated. Eliza lost all of her children to freedom. This c. 1848 daguerreotype of Eliza, mother of Bishop James Augustine Healy, is reproduced courtesy of Dr. Thomas Riley, second great-nephew of Bishop James Augustine Healy. (Courtesy of Dr. Thomas Riley.)

In 1858, Mary Bradley immigrated to New Hampshire from County Kerry, Ireland, with her six children after the death of her husband and three-month-old son John. Surviving the Great Famine and knowing that she would not stay alive or provide for her children as a widow, she believed the family's journey to America would provide a safer place to live. Destiny proved otherwise. In her lifetime, Mary lost all of her children except one, Denis, to death. Here, Mary is featured in a stained-glass window in St. Joseph Cathedral as an Irish woman wearing mourning clothes. (Courtesy of Gerald Durette.)

In 1884, seven dioceses in New England were independently established. This image is an archival reproduction of the original and only extant photograph of New England's bishops attending the Third Plenary Council in Baltimore. Pictured are, from left to right, (sitting) Bishop James Augustine Healy, Portland, Maine; Bishop Lawrence Stephen McMahon, Hartford, Connecticut; Bishop Louis de Goesbriand, Burlington, Vermont; Archbishop John Joseph Williams, Boston, Massachusetts; Bishop Patrick Thomas O'Reilly, Springfield, Massachusetts; and Bishop Thomas Francis Hendricken, Providence, Rhode Island; (standing) Bishop Denis Mary Bradley, Manchester, New Hampshire. (Courtesy of Gerald Durette.)

Subdivisions, called deaneries, were established to manage smaller areas within the diocese. In Exodus 18:17–26, Moses listens to good advice from his father-in-law to promote and rely on leadership among capable men. This marble sculpture of Moses portrays his muscular physique holding the tablets on which the Decalogue was written by the hand of God. What appear to be horns extending from his head is the artistic expression of the light that emanated from his countenance when he was in the presence of the Almighty. (Author's collection.)

In Chapter XXI of the Holy Rule, St. Benedict explains his administration plan in these words: "If the brotherhood is large, let brethren of good repute and holy life be chosen from among them and be appointed Deans, and let them take care of their deaneries in everything according to the commandments of God and the directions of their Abbot. Let such be chosen Deans as the Abbot may safely trust to share his burden. Let them not be chosen for their rank, but for the merit of their life and their wisdom and knowledge." This scriptural and monastic practice soon found its way into diocesan pastoral practicality. Originally, deaneries were named for the largest populated cities in the state: East and West Manchester, Berlin, Dover, Franconia, Laconia, Lebanon, Nashua, and Salem. Bishop John McCormack enhanced the identity of deaneries by closely aligning them with the state's nine territorial districts. Realizing New Hampshire's historic reputation for being a place of athleticism, recreation, and global significance for its natural beauty, the contemporary church associates herself with the grandeur of God's creation from the White Mountains to the seacoast. (Author's collection.)

Two

Amoskeag Deanery
A Good Fish Place

Our Lady of the Cedars is a Melkite-Greek Catholic church. In 1930, Lebanese immigrants, who shared a religious heritage, petitioned Manchester's third bishop to found their own church. Divine Liturgy was celebrated in their new house of worship 26 years later. Parish growth through the next quarter-century necessitated moving to a larger edifice. A Roman Catholic church became available and was acquired by the Melkite Catholics where religious life continues. (Courtesy of Our Lady of the Cedars Archives.)

Amoskeag, from the native Pennacook word *Namoskeag*, translates to "good fish place." The Merrimack River streaming through Amoskeag Deanery provided a plentiful supply of migrating sturgeon, blue back herring, and salmon. *Merrimack*, meaning "swift water place," identifies portions of the river between Manchester, New Hampshire, and Lowell, Massachusetts. (Courtesy of the Ken Francher collection.)

In 1848, Rev. William McDonald began his ministry in Manchester as the city's first resident priest, accepting Bishop John Bernard Fitzpatrick's assignment from Boston. Eventually, Father McDonald successfully increased religious resources necessary to establish the initial and legitimate identity of Catholics in New Hampshire's largest urban settlement. Fighting against anti-Catholic hostility until the very end, he had served his church and God's people tirelessly for 37 years when he entered eternal life, hearing the words, "Well done, good and faithful servant." (Courtesy of the Portland Diocesan Archives.)

In 1848, St. Anne's was established as the first Catholic church in Manchester. On his arrival, Father McDonald was immediately confronted with organized efforts to displace an estimated 500 Catholics from their urban neighborhoods, where they lived close to employment and necessary services, to the outer edge of town. He secured land closer to center city only to be hoodwinked by contractors who used inferior building materials. The structure only lasted four years and had to be rebuilt. The campus shown in this original photograph includes the church, convent, rectory, and school. (Courtesy of Richard Duckoff, Manchester Historical Association trustee.)

With an increase in Irish and French Canadian Catholics between 1848 and 1864, Father McDonald was instructed to build a larger church. Patrick Charles Keely, a preeminent architect from New York, was employed to design the edifice. Construction began in 1865 and was completed in 1869. The parish was dedicated to St. Joseph. In the latter half of the 19th century, architect Keely designed an estimated 600 churches and hundreds of other institutional buildings for the Roman Catholic Church in America and Canada. (Courtesy of the Patrick Charles Keely Society.)

This 1869 sketch shows the original interior of St. Joseph Church. Two stained-glass windows original to the church, depicting St. Anne and the Holy Family's flight into Egypt, were transferred and are extant in the Chapel of the Most Blessed Sacrament. (Courtesy of *Manchester Union Leader*.)

The Diocese of Manchester became independent in 1884, and St. Joseph Church became St. Joseph Cathedral, the spiritual heart of the new see. The first bishop renovated the original church by enlarging the sanctuary, introducing frescoes of the apostles between the supporting arches, and enhancing the altar with a marble reredos. He installed Stations of the Cross in the nave. The cathedral featured scripturally sound Tyolese stained-glass windows that served as teachers for a largely illiterate congregation. A Tiffany altar stone and oil paintings created by local artists completed the sanctuary. (Courtesy of the Manchester Diocesan Archives.)

This 1969 photograph of the cathedral's renovation reveals the absence of former architectural appointments. The sixth bishop of Manchester modernized the interior of the cathedral by destroying the original marble reredos, plastering over frescoes, and removing the Stations of the Cross. He installed carpet and painted the walls a neutral cream color. (Courtesy of the Manchester Diocesan Archives.)

Under the direction of Manchester's 10th bishop, the cathedral was restored and renovated. Holy Trinity Church in Boston, designed and built by the same architect who built Manchester's St. Joseph Church in 1865, closed. Providentially, the reredos, statues, side altars, and Stations of the Cross previously adorning that church became available to the cathedral, restoring the sanctuary and nave more closely to their original transcendence. Msgr. Anthony R. Frontiero, 18th rector of the cathedral, completed restoration of the Chapel of the Most Blessed Sacrament and initiated renovation of the cathedral. (Courtesy of Gerald Durette.)

Pictured here is the Reverend Mother Frances Xavier Warde, foundress of the Sisters of Mercy in America. The Sisters of Mercy were respectfully known as the Catholic Church's departments of health, education, and welfare. On March 14, 1858, Bishop Francis Patrick McFarland from Rhode Island released a few Sisters of Mercy to establish a mission in Manchester. The sisters were warned of threatening anti-Catholic fanatics who swore that "no woman wearing the religious garb shall ever enter the territory." They learned about an 1854 incident in which a Manchester mob drove Catholics from their homes and dragged the sick from their beds to the streets, burning their furniture. Into this hostile environment five Sisters of Mercy, the first women religious in New Hampshire, arrived in Manchester on July 16, 1858, the feast of Our Lady of Mount Carmel. (Courtesy of Manchester Historical Association.)

The Sisters of Mercy were met at the Manchester Boston & Maine (B&M) Railroad station, featured here, by Reverend McDonald and welcoming Catholics. Transported by hired carriage, they arrived at their convent to find prepared food and flowers. They immediately entered the chapel, where the Blessed Sacrament awaited their prayers of thanksgiving for a safe journey and, on this day, a nonviolent homecoming. (Courtesy of Manchester Historical Association.)

BANDMASTER WALTER DIGNAM.

Manchester resident Walter Dignam registered for military service on September 3, 1861. On September 18, at age 33, he answered the call to arms. As one of an estimated 100,000 bandsmen, 2nd Lt. Walter Dignam achieved distinguished service as bandmaster of the New Hampshire 4th Regiment Volunteers. Leading troops with resound of brass instruments and keeping cadence with drums, he and his band eased the drudgery of long marches and bolstered the spirits of weary soldiers. Dignam survived the Battles of Antietam and Gettysburg to muster out on September 16, 1862. His monthlong journey from Hilton Head, South Carolina, returned him to New Hampshire, where he became music director at St. Anne's Parish and rose to national leadership in the American Brass Band Movement, which began in New England. Walter Dignam died on April 22, 1891. Bishop Bradley laid him to rest among the honorable graves of fellow Civil War comrades in St. Joseph Cemetery. (Courtesy of Manchester Historical Association.)

Just as the city of Manchester is separated east from west by the Merrimack River, so too were the populations of largely French and Irish immigrants who came to work in the mills. Choosing to retain their respective traditions and languages, laity, priests, and sisters petitioned the Diocese of Portland to establish their own ethnic churches, cemeteries, and schools. In the years leading up to and closely following the turn of the century, seven churches, built within blocks of each other, accommodated Irish, French, German, and Polish Catholics. In anticipation of the first bishop being of French descent, in 1880, Msgr. Pierre Hevey constructed Ste. Marie Church, the largest French parish in Manchester. (Courtesy of the Msgr. Charles DesRuisseaux collection.)

Ukrainian immigrants began arriving in Manchester in 1884. Bishop Bradley granted permission for congregants to worship in St. Joseph Cathedral, where Eastern-rite religious life continued until the Protection of Mary Church was built in 1907. The church was dedicated on October 18, 1908, by the Most Reverend Soter Ortunsky. Glory to Jesus Christ! Glory Forever! Слава Ісусу Христу! Слава на Віки! (Courtesy of the Protection of Mary Church.)

As Manchester's shepherd concerned with the spiritual welfare of his flock, Bishop Bradley appealed to Abbot Hilary Pfraengle, OSB, of St. Mary's Benedictine Abbey in Newark, New Jersey. Bishop Bradley influenced the abbot to consider the plight of Catholics attending Protestant churches because there were no German-speaking priests in the diocese. Responding to the sacramental needs of New Hampshire's German Catholics, a papal decree dated November 27, 1887, authorized construction of a parish for English- and German-speaking Catholics in West Manchester under the patronage of St. Raphael. This photograph of First Communicants 75 years after its founding provides evidence that the multiethnic parish is still flourishing. (Courtesy of St. Raphael Parish Archives.)

This photograph was taken at the dedication of Saint Anselm College, founded in 1889 by Abbot Hilary Pfraengle, OSB, of St. Mary's Benedictine Abbey, Newark, New Jersey, and the Right Reverend Denis Mary Bradley, bishop of Manchester. Bishop Bradley is seated in the center of the

first row, with Abbot Hilary to the left of him. The third-oldest Catholic college in New England is named in honor of Saint Anselm, archbishop of Canterbury. (Courtesy of Msgr. Wilfrid H. Paradis Archives and Special Collections, Geisel Library, Saint Anselm College.)

This young member of St. George's Parish is prepared to receive his first Holy Communion. St. George Church was dedicated on April 1, 1890, by Bishop Denis Bradley as a French parish on the east side of Manchester. The majority of its members worked in the mills, located within walking distance of the parish. Making ends meet with minimum wages for long hours of dangerous millwork, the French community contributed money and labor to build the church, which served the faithful for more than a century. (Courtesy of Ken Francher collection.)

This weekly newspaper dedicated to the Blessed Virgin Mary contained her Latin title, *Monstra Te Esse Matrem*, which means "To Present Yourself as a Mother." This newspaper was published by Steven O'Connell of Manchester between September 7, 1892, and August 28, 1893. *New Hampshire Catholic* was the premier information source for literate Catholics. The newspaper informed readers of parish and diocesan events not published in secular newsprint. (Courtesy of Manchester Historical Association.)

St. Patrick Parish, founded in 1898 on the west side of Manchester, established an ethnic home for Irish Catholics. Irish immigrants, a minority Catholic population living in a predominantly French community, built their church on a hill overlooking the Merrimack River and the expansive length of mills that provided minimum income in exchange for dangerously hard labor. (Author's collection.)

United by God's infinite participation in the history of man, each bishop lives in a finite period of world culture that prompts his actions, defines his governance, and informs his faith, incontrovertible with his local, national, and international experience. Considering his mortality and anticipating eternal repose for his succeeding brother bishops, the Right Reverend Denis Bradley designed and constructed a crypt located directly below the bishop's cathedra. This consecrated enclosure is among the first places visited by newly appointed bishops. In this vault, the first five prelates of Manchester lie securely within walls thick enough to qualify as a bomb shelter. Here, thousands of visitors, including Catholic teachers, students, historians, and non-Catholic guests, enter the crypt and experience its sacred silence. Pausing in prayer, they bow in gratitude and respect. In this sacred place, a singular teaching moment enables visitors to grasp the lifetimes of these men and reflect on the years during which they served the church. (Courtesy of the Manchester Diocese.)

As the casket of Bishop Bradley reached the doors of his beloved cathedral in December 1903, a coordinated plan throughout Manchester brought the city to silence. The clip of horse hooves drawing streetcars stopped. Deafening noises of mill machines ceased, including those in the cloth shop shown in this photograph. The only sound, save a baby's cry or a horse's whinny, was the two-minute clanging of every church bell in Manchester, Catholic and Protestant, tolling for the loss of saintly Bishop Denis Bradley. (Courtesy of Manchester Historical Association.)

In their thanksgiving for the strength of Bishop Bradley's character, Catholics used the state's strongest natural resource, granite, to erect a monument in the cathedral courtyard between the Chapel of the Most Blessed Sacrament and the episcopal residence. Rising to a Celtic cross, symbols of the Four Evangelists give witness to Bishop Bradley's image and, eventually, to the first four bishops of Manchester. (Courtesy of the Ken Francher collection.)

Le Travailleur

(Weekly devoted exclusively to the recording and the promotion of Franco-American cultural activities)

Jeudi, le 1 juillet 1948

hateaubriand

D'HIER

BRIAND

gaden

"Je sème l'or"
evise des Chateaubriand)

ort de Chateaubriand, nous
émoire du génial écrivain,
place est si grande dans la
sans lui.
ndérante, il lui a donné un
sanctifiée, et qui a permis

uer Chateaubriand: dans la
a fait ample connaissance
largement.
, dans la rue des Juifs, le
olent orage équinoxial que
a cathédrale.
né d'Auguste de Chateau-
aient eu dix enfants, dont
François René et fut

Chateaubriand n'a garde de manquer au rendez-vous. Il y a cinq ou six convives. La conversation roule sur la France. Le général montre une clé de la Bastille, à la fois un souvenir et un symbole.

A dix heures du soir, Chateaubriand prend congé de Washington, décidé à poursuivre son voyage et sa difficile exploration en terre américaine.

A partir de ce jour, et jusqu'au 10 décembre 1791, Chateaubriand parcourt l'Amérique. Il part pour New York, va en pèlerinage à Boston, où il salue le premier champ de bataille de la liberté américaine, retourne à New York, remonte l'Hudson en bateau, jusqu'à Albany, se dirige vers le Niagara, parcourt le Labrador, la région des lacs, les prairies du centre, la Louisiane, descend l'Ohio, puis le Mississippi, gagne la Floride, revient chez les Natchez, retourne à Baltimore par le désert.

Il ébauche "Atala", écrit sur ses genoux l'Histoire d'une nation sauvage du Canada."

La lecture fortuite d'un journal apprend à Chateaubriand l'arrestation de Louis XVI. Un sursaut de patriotisme, de civisme et de royalisme s'empare de lui. Il décide de rentrer en France. Au début de l'hiver, le 10 décembre 1791, Chateaubriand prend la mer.

Il n'a pas découvert le passage du N.-O. Mais il va pouvoir écrire Les Natchez, Le Voyage en Amérique, et consignera, plus tard, les péripéties de son "exploration" dans ses Mémoires d'outre-tombe.

Au reste, il semble prouvé que Chateaubriand a apporté beaucoup de vérité et beaucoup de fiction dans la relation de son voyage en Amérique. Peut-être vaut-il mieux, au point de vue littéraire, qu'il en soit ainsi.

*   *   *

Chateaubriand débarque en France le 2 janvier 1792, en

Lettre de Paris

Robert Schuman et le "sex-appeal" — Le romancier-trompette — Abondance de prodiges — Jeanne d'Arc tuée une fois de plus.

par Fernand BERTAL

M. Robert Schuman, ex-président du Conseil des Ministres, est un homme d'une extrême simplicité de moeurs. Il déteste les honneurs et quitte fréquemment l'Hôtel Matignon par une porte dérobée, afin de ne pas être suivi par les policiers chargés de le protéger.

Sa distraction favorite est d'aller se promener sur les quais, le long des éventaires des bouquinistes. Il rentre ensuite à son cabinet de travail avec plusieurs volumes sous le bras.

Il arrive que les gardes ne le reconnaissent pas et veulent l'empêcher de rentrer chez lui!

Dans l'intimité, M. Schuman est fort économe aussi bien de ses propres deniers que de ceux de l'Etat. Il n'a qu'une bonne et prend des repas mo-

La quere
canadie

De l

Novembre 1869:
et notamment en Fra
engendrait d'acrimon
à l'opportunité de cet
ques qui soutenaient
nécessité théologique
niers se trouvait Lou
l'ultramontanisme, le
Mgr Gaume. C'était
d'autres d'inimitié
moins grand journali

Sur ces entrefai
protestait violemmen
que de l'infaillibilité
deux coups, l'évêque
de patte à Louis Veu
y eût — d'avoir prêt
Ce dernier vint 1

This semiweekly newspaper was printed between 1874 and 1892, when it ceased temporarily. Between 1932 and 1978, *Le Travailleur* was published simultaneously in Manchester, New Hampshire, and Linwood, Massachusetts. It served as an essential news source for French Catholics. During its 45-year run, it was published weekly and distributed throughout New England. (Courtesy of the Manchester Diocesan Archives.)

Edmund Pinard realized the hardship Catholics endured rowing across treacherous Piscataquog River currents to attend Holy Mass at Ste. Marie Parish. In 1905, he purchased 12 acres west of the river, built homes for his family, and donated a parcel of land where St. Edmund Church was dedicated on January 8, 1915, by Bishop George Albert Guertin. (Author's collection.)

Students graduating from St. Edmund School in the 1950s carry on the pre–Vatican Council tradition of separating boys and girls during official church events. After serving Catholics for nearly a century, the diocese sold the church. Currently Shiloh Community Church, a vibrant Christian congregation, occupies the church, where religious life continues. (Courtesy of Manchester Historical Association.)

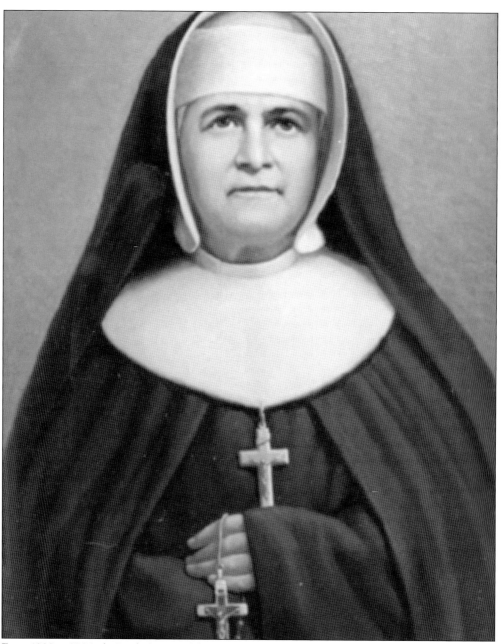

From 1908 to 2006, the Little Sisters of the Holy Family humbly cared for priests. In domestic service to the diocese, they tended vegetable gardens, cooked meals, cleaned rectories, cared for ill and aging bishops and priests, and provided hospitality for guests grand and casual. Foundress Mother Marie-Léonie instilled in her sisters the charism of "the incarnation and the manifestation of the face of the Servant Christ, present in his priests." (Courtesy of the Manchester Diocesan Archives.)

US Army private Henry John Sweeney, member of St. Raphael Parish, was the first soldier from Manchester to perish in World War I. Sweeney joined the Sheridan Guard on April 13, 1917, serving in the 52nd Brigade, 26th Division. Merging with the 103rd Infantry Regiment, he fought on the front lines in Champagne-Marne, Aisne-Marne, St. Mihel, Meuse-Argonne, Ile de France, and Lorraine. On February 18, 1918, he was mortally wounded in Soisson, France. His remains were buried in France and transferred to Manchester when hostilities ended. This bronze bust created by Catholic sculptor Lucien Gosselin memorializes his sacrifice. (Courtesy of Sweeney Post Archives.)

On May 13, 1919, Bishop George Albert Guertin addresses Catholics welcoming home the Sheridan Guard after World War I. Gov. John Bartlett and Mayor Moise Verrette of Manchester are seated to the left of the bishop. Rev. John J. Lyons is seated to the right of the bishop. Catholics on the dais include Nashua mayor Henri Burque, sailor Thomas Fecteau, and soldier Philip Fleming. Banners indicate that 719 New Hampshire individuals served in the American Civil War and 335 served in World War I. The star beneath the figure 110 records the number of New Hampshire citizens who perished serving their country. (Courtesy of the Manchester Diocesan Archives.)

Centered in the baptistry of St. Raphael Parish, this stained-glass work *For God and Country* was acquired from St. Bridget Parish, Chicago. Transporting, cleaning, and restoring the window was accomplished by parishioners, New Hampshire Department of Catholic War Veterans, and Catholic War Veterans Auxiliary. The image of Christ, Lord of Armies, extends his consoling embrace to a sailor, soldier, and airman flanked by unfurling US and Papal flags. Boot prints lead to the Prince of Peace. Hemispheric globes define a world divided by war; however, reconciled in the sphere, a unified world is depicted under the outstretched wings of a victorious eagle. Twelve medallions depict military symbols of the Air Force, Army, Navy, Marines, and youth corps. (Courtesy of St. Raphael Parish.)

In 1922, Irene Farley began her apostolic work of financially supporting the education of aspiring priests in missions throughout the world. She founded the Missionary Rosebushes of St. Therese and raised hundreds of thousands of dollars for seminarians. On December 8, 1927, in Trichinopoly, India, the first two proteges of the Rosebushes, future bishop Jacob Mendoça and Maria-Joseph Chinnappen, were ordained to the priesthood. Following the death of Irene Farley, the Sisters Adorers of the Precious Blood accepted the intention of her ministry and continue to promote the ordination of seminarians in missions worldwide. (Courtesy of Sisters Adorers of the Precious Blood Archives.)

This 1935 photograph shows the contemplatives Sisters Adorers of the Precious Blood. The venerable Mother Catherine Aurelia Caouette, a French Canadian, founded the order in 1861. In 1898, Bishop Bradley welcomed their cloistered presences to the Diocese of Manchester, where they continue to pray fervently for bishops, laity, priests, and vocations. "May the Divine Blood be your joy, your strength, your hope," said the foundress. (Courtesy of the Portland Diocesan Archives.)

Polish Day was celebrated annually with picnics and performances in the city park that honors Kazimierz Michał Władysław Wiktor Pułaski, the military hero who fought for Polish and American Independence. On October 15, 1939, Polish Boy and Girl Scouts and the Polish Drill Team pose in front of the Casimir Pulaski statue. (Courtesy of the Jean Dubois collection.)

The Fraternite Sacerdotale was a pontifical order of clerics who ministered to secular priests. They managed retreat houses and rest homes in France, Italy, and Canada. When Germans soldiers occupied Paris in World War II, they took over most religious convents and monasteries. The superior of Father Glaude's residence retained the Americans' passports. Had their documents been shown to the occupying forces, the priests would not have been detained in prisoner of war camps, because the United States was not yet involved in the European war. These priests survived their incarceration and were returned to New Hampshire, where they were incardinated. Fr. Arthur Glaude and his brother priests suffered for the rest of their lives from the torture, cold, and lack of food in the prisoner of war camps. This only extant image of Father Glaude graces the narthex of St. Anthony Parish. (Author's collection.)

"....with Christ I hang upon the cross, and yet I am alive; or rather, not I; it is Christ that lives in me."

(Galatians 2:20)

Rev. Arthur E. Glaude who served this Parish from 1945 to 1970.

47

St. Catherine of Siena Parish members Joseph and Bridget Geisel directed their substantial resources toward the values they cherished most: family; belief in Our Lord, Jesus Christ; Catholic education; and civic leadership. Statesman and financier Joseph Geisel served as Manchester city alderman, postmaster, state senator, and representative. Among the many legacies for which he is remembered is his devotion to Saint Anselm College as a trustee, where he endowed the library that bears his name and honors his generosity. He is shown here in 1960 laying the cornerstone for Geisel Library, located prominently across from the abbey church. (Courtesy of Msgr. Wilfrid H. Paradis Archives and Special Collections, Geisel Library, Saint Anselm College.)

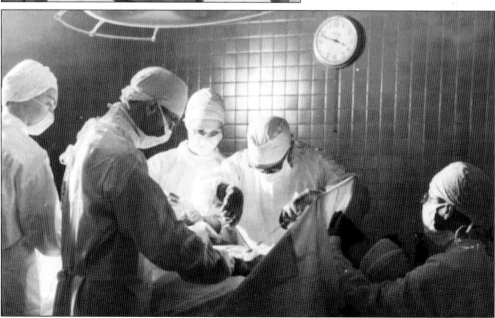

The origin of Catholic Medical Center is rooted in the devotion of religious community members determined to provide healthcare to Manchester's residents. The hospital's story began in 1858 with the arrival of Mother Mary Gonzaga, one of the original Sisters of Mercy from Dublin, Ireland. Her intention to establish a hospital sponsored by a religious community was accomplished in 1892 with the opening of Sacred Heart Hospital. (Courtesy of Catholic Medical Center Archives.)

In August 1956, ten young women left their family homes in New Hampshire and Massachusetts to become postulants in the religious community of the Sisters of Holy Cross. On Monday, February 11, 1957, having completed six months of postulancy, these women entered St. Augustine Church wearing wedding gowns signifying they are brides of Christ. The young woman pictured kneels at the altar rail in St. Augustine Church in Manchester receiving the religious habit presented to her by Bishop Matthew F. Brady. On this day, each one has given her heart to God. (Courtesy of Manchester Historical Association.)

"O Lord our God, how glorious is your name in all the earth!" These first words spoken as Abbot Joseph John Gerry, OSB, accepts his assignment as auxiliary bishop of Manchester are his hymn of praise and thanksgiving, as they were for Jesus. Ordained on the feast day and quoting Saint Anselm of Canterbury, Bishop Joseph petitions God "that I may so know you and love you that I may rejoice in you." Indeed! Since his first monastic vows professed in 1948, the church of Manchester and Portland has rejoiced with him in the Lord. (Photograph by Aurel Stuart; courtesy of Msgr. Wilfrid H. Paradis Archives and Special Collection, Geisel Library, Saint Anselm College.)

The diocese responded to the appeal of Pope John XXIII for the church to come to the aid of people in Latin America. In 1965, Bishop Ernest Primeau appointed two priests and two sisters to Cartago, Colombia. In the successive years, lay missionaries and Peace Corps volunteers have served people of all ages in Colombia by providing the essentials of life—food, shelter, clean water, and academic and religious education. (Courtesy of the Manchester Diocesan Archives.)

Preceding the technology information age, information to clergy was transmitted by a diocesan newsletter called *Inter Nos*, meaning "among us." The format included clarification of religious disciplines and protocols for liturgical seasons and announcements of various diocesan events. The newsletter promoted opportunities for vocation awareness and provided guidance in planning liturgies and faith formation events. Editors directed pastors with practical advice: "lock the rectory doors, thieves are everywhere." (Courtesy of the Manchester Diocesan Archives.)

March 1978

Inter Nos...

Published for the Clergy of the
Diocese of Manchester, N.H.

HOLY WEEK, 1978...

Holy Week begins this year on Palm Sunday, March 19 through the Easter Vigil, March 25. The Chancery Office refers you to the liturgical directives for Holy Week published in past issues of the Chancery Bulletin.

HOLY THURSDAY: MASS OF THE CHRISM...

The Mass of the Chrism will be concelebrated at the Cathedral on Holy Thursday morning, March 23 at 9:30 A.M.

In the revised rite for Holy Thursday morning, the Mass of the Chrism, at which the oils are blessed, manifests the communion of the priests with their bishop. Bishop Gendron extends a cordial invitation to all priests of the Diocese, if pastorally feasible, to concelebrate the Mass with him.

Each concelebrant is asked to bring his own amice, plain alb, cincture and stole. Arrangements will be made for the clergy to vest downstairs in the Cathedral Hall. The procession will begin promptly at 9:15. (Priests who concelebrate the Mass of the Chrism or celebrate a Mass for the convenience of the faithful may concelebrate again at the evening Mass.)

The Holy Oils will be distributed after the ceremonies between 11:00-12:00 Noon at the Cathedral Rectory, and again in the afternoon between 1:30-3:30 P.M.

THE CELEBRATION OF THE EASTER VIGIL...

Parishes are reminded that the Easter Vigil, which is to be the first liturgical celebration of Easter, should not be celebrated until sunset at the earliest. For your information, the weather bureau in Concord advises that sunset on March 25th is at 6:04 P.M.

FUNERAL RITES DURING THE EASTER TRIDUUM...

"...A funeral Mass is not to be celebrated during the Paschal Triduum nor on the morning of Holy Thursday...If funeral rites take place on these days, it is fitting that there be a Liturgy of the Word with a rite of commendation and farewell as provided in the Funeral Ritual. Whereas singing is permitted during the celebration (of such a rite), the distribution of communion is not..." (Newsletter of the Bishops' Committee on the Liturgy, February-March 1976).

PRESBYTERIUM MEETING AT ST. ANSELM'S APRIL 18...

A meeting of the presbyterium of the Diocese will take place Tuesday, April 18 at 10:30 A.M. in the North Lounge of the Cushing Center at St. Anselm's College.

Diocese of Manchester • Office of Communications • 153 Ash Street • Manchester, N.H. 03105

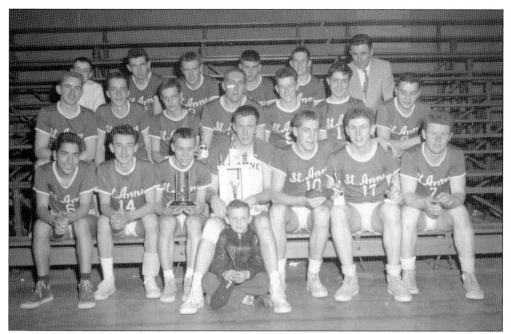

Catholic athletic competition taught young men the values of good sportsmanship, as well as the importance of working together as a team, celebrating success, and displaying good character at losses. This 1960s St. Anne basketball team exemplifies team unity at the conclusion of a successful season. (Courtesy of Manchester Historical Association.)

Cheerleading was and is an expression of athleticism and skillful energy. These 1960s athletes embody confidence, precision drill movements, and a spirit of love for their school. (Courtesy of Manchester Historical Association.)

Extending from 19th-century women religious, St. Vincent de Paul Society, and countless individuals who fed the hungry, clothed the naked, and sheltered the homeless, Catholic Charities became a funded ministry of the diocese in 1945. The first official food bank collected and stored food in a two-by-four-foot shed. Volunteers, protected by good samaritan legislation, served the poor out of a Winnebago camper on a back alley in Manchester. In addition to his pastoral duties, Bishop Matthew F. Brady tapped Rev. John Moulin to conduct a financial drive to build nursing homes throughout the diocese. Layman Paul Coleman was hired as the first director of Catholic Charities, and Margaret Corbett served as secretary. This photograph of Bishop Primeau and Catholic Charities officials celebrates 20 years of the diocesan ministry. (Courtesy of Manchester Historical Association.)

Founded in 1897 as an auxiliary of the Knights of Columbus, Daughters of Isabella is an organization of Catholic laywomen based on the principles of unity, friendship, and charity. Known as "circles of friends," members strive to know one another better and pursue good in society by centralizing resources that support nonprofits, provide scholarships, and contribute to parish life. Keeping their decades-long tradition, these Daughters of Isabella are making 950 pork pies for families celebrating Thanksgiving Day. (Author's collection.)

This Good Shepherd statue invites the faithful to visit and honor the sixth and eighth bishops of the Diocese of Manchester reposing in St. Joseph Cemetery. Bishops Ernest Primeau and Leo O'Neil rest in peace with their brother priests and among the faithful on the sanctified grounds dedicated to Manchester's bishops and clergy. (Author's collection.)

Following the abbatial blessing of Abbot Gerald McCarthy, OSB, on September 4, 1963, *Anselmian News* reported that many were shocked when Richard Cardinal Cushing exclaimed the following: "This is an institution without a heart. Just as the human body cannot survive without a heart, neither can this monastery and college survive without a heart. As you know, the heart of a monastery is an adequate abbey church, and you people don't have a heart!" Cardinal Cushing encouraged construction of the abbey church with a pledge of $500,000, almost half the cost of construction. (Photograph by Aurel Stuart; courtesy of Msgr. Wilfrid H. Paradis Archives and Special Collection, Geisel Library, Saint Anselm College.)

Ancient church history extends through the centuries. Gerald Cardinal Lacroix was born on July 27, 1957, in Saint-Hilaire-de-Dorset in the Archdiocese of Quebec. His family moved to Manchester, where he attended St. Anthony Elementary School, Trinity High School, and Saint Anselm College. He is the current archbishop of Quebec and primate of Canada. In this photograph, he is meeting with members of the Ancient Equestrian Order of the Holy Sepulchre of Jerusalem. (Courtesy of the Msgr. Charles DesRuisseaux collection.)

Three

CAPITAL DEANERY
HARMONY BETWEEN DISPUTANT TOWNS

In 1858, Bernadette Soubirous was gathering firewood when a "lady" spoke to her in a cave near Lourdes, France. Pope Pius IX approved veneration to Our Lady of Lourdes in 1870. Nineteen years following papal approval of adoration to this title attributed to Our Blessed Mother, Catholics in Pittsfield honored her patronage. The mission church, founded in 1887 was blessed by Bishop Bradley in 1889. (Courtesy of Rev. John MacKenzie, pastor Our Lady of Lourdes Parish.)

The Very Reverend John Barry, a priest in the Diocese of Portland, was named pastor of St. John the Evangelist Parish in Concord. He served Bishop Bradley as his vicar general and theologian at the Third Plenary Council. He counseled Pres. Franklin Pierce. Father Barry was struck and killed by a streetcar in New York City on November 14, 1900. He was so respected at the time of his death that every Christian church in Concord published tributes praising his character and mourning his loss. Like the city, named for a settlement between two disputing towns, Father Barry's life brought people of differing traditions together. (Courtesy of the Portland Diocesan Archives.)

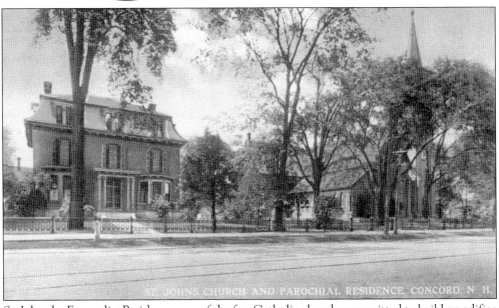

St. John the Evangelist Parish was one of the few Catholic churches permitted to build an edifice on a New Hampshire city main street. Construction of a brick episcopal residence and St. Mary's Parochial School at the same prominent address in 1865 was remarkable. St. John's became a crucial spiritual resource for the minority of Catholic state representatives and senators who traveled from their respective towns at such distances that it was frequently impossible for them to return home in time for Sunday Holy Mass. (Courtesy of the Ken Francher collection.)

In 1850, the Suncook Valley Railroad revolutionized development of a mostly agricultural area into an industrial center. In 1861, Suncook was designated a mission of St. John the Evangelist Parish in Concord. Rev. Jean-Baptiste Richer from Manitoba founded the Suncook parish in 1871, naming the church in honor of his patron saint. The Societé St. Jean-Baptiste de Suncook is seen in this photograph celebrating St. Jean-Baptiste Day in front of the church. Formed to protect the culture, language, and political concerns of Francophones, the societé originated in Quebec and extended into America as the French population joined ranks with these patriots. (Courtesy of St. John the Baptist Parish Archives.)

Sisters of Holy Cross and Seven Dolors educated students in Suncook as early as 1888. The student population increased, and by 1910, the school occupied shared space with the convent. This photograph of 1913 graduates represents the calm of peacetime pomp and circumstance. Students provide a splendid display of feminine accomplishment and pride. (Courtesy of St. John the Baptist Parish Archives.)

The 1915 graduating class at St. Jean-Baptiste Parish features young adults confidently posed with their certificates in hand. Additional certificates awarded to those not present rest on top of stacked hardbound books. Note the generous bouquets of flowers presented to the girls and the academic medal awarded to the young man. (Courtesy of St. John the Baptist Parish Archives.)

The parochial school associated with Holy Rosary Parish in Hooksett was founded in 1891 by Rev. A.J. Simard as a bilingual elementary school. It is unclear who the earliest teachers were. The French Canadian Sisters of Holy Cross took charge of the school for 28 years. The parish was not large enough to support a convent, which meant the sisters traveled from Suncook every day. Despite the hardship that required students to work during the academic year to sustain their families, the school received state-approved certification. Sisters of Mercy replaced the Holy Cross Sisters for four years until the 1936 flood destroyed the school. (Courtesy of Holy Rosary Parish Archives.)

Holy Rosary Parish in Hooksett was founded in 1886 as a mission of St. John the Evangelist Parish in Concord. In addition to an abundance of fish harvested from the Merrimack River, several cross-river ferries provided transportation and jobs. In 1936, the same river that benefitted settlers flooded, disrupting daily life for years. This photograph shows parishioners watching helplessly as their church basement is flooded and the structure is threatened by rising waters. The river torrent rendered the original edifice structurally unsound. The present church stands on higher ground on the main street of Hooksett. Holy Rosary is the only parish in the diocese with its cemetery located directly adjacent to the church. (Courtesy of Holy Rosary Parish Archives.)

St. Peter's was originally a mission in the north end of Concord under the jurisdiction of St. John the Evangelist Church. The parish was established in 1906 to serve Irish Catholic immigrants who found work as firefighters, mill workers, and granite miners. Short-lived employment with one of the numerous quarries in proximity to Concord provided decent wages until the Depression years. St. Peter's Parish welcomed the faithful for 112 years. (Courtesy of the Ken Francher collection.)

This photograph indicative of early-American church furnishings features Advent decorations and wooden benches preceding cushioned pews and padded kneelers. Emerging from nearly 40 years as a mission, Our Lady of Lourdes was established as a parish in 1926. In its founding year, the parish adopted the mission of St. Joseph in Northwood into its protective, spiritual care. The presence of the Catholic community in Pittsfield was strengthened when the episcopal residence was built next to the church on a hill overlooking the Suncook River. The congregation supported a convent for the Franciscan Sisters of the Atonement who taught religious education for 23 years. (Courtesy of Our Lady of Lourdes Parish Archives.)

In 1874, John Leddy was the only Catholic and Democrat serving in the state legislature. Leddy, a highly visible and vocal Catholic, was elected before the proviso against nonprotestants was removed from the state constitution. He was one of the founders of St. Joseph Mission in Epping, where he is buried with several Civil War veterans and early Catholics. His legacy includes development of his farmland into a single-dwelling adult housing community known as Leddy Fields and an entire block of permanent business buildings. (Courtesy of Brian Nelson Burford, New Hampshire state archivist.)

The first French Canadian state senator, Joseph P. Chatel, was one of two Democrats in the 1899 Republican House and the first Catholic of French origin to be elected in any of the six New England states. Chatel became the successful proprietor of a liquor store in Manchester, enjoying wide acquaintances and popularity. (Courtesy of the Ken Francher collection.)

Mount St. Mary's Academy was founded by the Sisters of Mercy in 1909 on 300 acres of field and woodland in Hooksett. The grand structure sits atop one of the highest hills in the town with an envious view. It served as the oldest convent boarding school for girls in northern New England, accepting elementary and high school students. Charted in 1934, Mount St. Mary's became the first four-year women's college in New Hampshire. It's state-accredited curriculum offered a full range of academic, literary, and scientific courses. The college closed in 1978. A large sum of money from the sale of the college was donated to the literacy campaign in Nicaragua. (Courtesy of the Ken Francher collection.)

Francis Murphy was the first Catholic to be elected governor of New Hampshire. He won the Republican nomination in 1936 and narrowly again in 1938. Murphy was chairman of the Committee on Electric Power Supply and a longtime member of the New Hampshire State National Guard. During his first term, his shoe manufacturing business grew to 12 plants, becoming the largest labor employer in New Hampshire. Murphy retired from but remained active in politics. He founded WMUR AM, WMUR FM, and WMUR TV in Manchester. (Courtesy of the Manchester Historical Association.)

Founded by humanitarian Gerolamo Emiliani (1486–1537), the Somascans are an international community of priests and sisters who devote their lives to the care of orphans and poor and distressed young boys and girls. In 1963, the Somascan fathers founded Pine Haven Boys Center, an accredited, licensed, private, nondenominational school serving an average of 20 boys in the first through eighth grades. The center is located on 100 acres of quietly protected fields and woodland. As an integral part of their academic education, students are supervised 24 hours each day and receive individual and group therapy. (Courtesy of Rev. Paul Riva, CRS.)

Donn Tibbetts, member of St. Joseph Cathedral, is seen here speaking as a member of Bishop Primeau's pastoral commission. After attending St. Joseph High School in Manchester, he graduated from the LaSalle Military Academy in Oakdale, New York, in 1948. As dean of the state house press corps, Tibbetts covered presidential primaries, state elections, the administrations of eight governors, and sessions of the nation's largest state legislature. Tibbetts wrote the "Under the State House Dome" column. *Union Leader*'s late publisher William Loeb, nationally known for his frank assessments, called Tibbetts "a man of great integrity, who reports things as he sees them, without fear or bias." (Courtesy of Manchester Historical Association.)

On Wednesday, January 3, 1973, the New Hampshire legislature appointed the state's first Catholic chaplain, Rev. Joseph Y. Beaulieu, pastor of St. Lawrence Parish in Goffstown. He opened the legislative session with the following prayer: "Lord God, it is so easy for me to be selfish and greedy and call it 'common sense.' I am often proud and sentimental and call it 'generosity.' Lord of my life, open up my narrow mind and show me that the goods of this world are tools You have given to help me live in Your world: That they must be used in many places, in many ways: to feed, to clothe, to teach, to please, to encourage, to repair, to rescue, to support, to protect, and now and then to make a dream come true. Lord, sharpen my perspective so that I make decisions with You in mind. Amen." (Courtesy of Phyllis Hanavan, administrative assistant, St. Lawrence Parish.)

Four

LAKES REGION DEANERY
SMILE OF THE GREAT SPIRIT

St. Joan of Arc Parish, Alton, founded in 1888, and St. Cecilia Parish, Wolfeboro, founded in 1896, merged to form a communion of saints. This merger established the first church in New Hampshire named for the most recently canonized American woman, St. Katharine Drexel, Sisters of the Blessed Sacrament (SBS). In May 2000, fire destroyed St. Joan of Arc Church. In the shock of their loss, parishioners wanted to build a new church at the same location. With biblical humor, their pastor, Rev. Richard Wegman, considered this possibility and said, "We could rebuild on this site, but we would have to rename the parish St. Blaise!" (Courtesy of St. Katharine Drexel Parish Archives.)

As early as 1844, missionary priests brought Holy Mass and the sacraments to Catholics settling in the Lakes Region, including the towns of Lakeport and Laconia. St. Joseph Parish in Laconia was established by Irish settlers who, with the help of Bishop Healy, built a church, which was destroyed by lightning in 1877. Bishop Healy's episcopal diary of Sunday, May 15, 1881, reads as follows: "The bishop (of Portland) dedicated the new church in Laconia & confirmed 20 persons mostly children. The church is large enough for a larger congregation, has a fine basement and is only $500 in debt. The school under the Sisters of Mercy is increasing in efficiency and in numbers." (Courtesy of the Ken Francher collection.)

The Roman-Gothic interior of Sacred Heart Parish in Laconia testifies to the artistic and architectural integrity of 19th-century attention to sacred spaces that beckon the faithful toward the transcendent. After 130 years of Holy Mass, baptisms, nuptials, funerals, and a thousand other occasions, this precious sanctuary is being restored as close as possible to its original splendor. (Courtesy of St. André Bissette Parish Archives.)

This photograph shows Sacred Heart Elementary School students performing a singing tribute to Our Lady's feast of the Assumption. In 1950, Pope Pius XII defined the taking of Our Lady to Heaven concluding her earthly life as dogma to be celebrated on August 15. Note the backdrop artwork depicting Our Lady ascending into celestial clouds. (Courtesy of St. André Bissette Parish Archives.)

SACRED HEART CHURCH, PAROCHIAL RESIDENCE, LACONIA, N. H.

By the late 19th century, industry in Laconia grew to include lumber, textile mills, hosiery and shoe manufacturers, and factories producing knitting machines and needles. Increasing labor needs of the region were met in large part by French Canadian immigrants. This population petitioned Bishop Bradley for a parish with a French-speaking pastor. In July 1891, the bishop of Manchester responded to their cultural and religious traditions by dedicating the second Catholic parish in Laconia to the Sacred Heart of Jesus. (Courtesy of St. André Bissette Parish Archives.)

Vacationers from far and wide came to swing and sway with Sammy Kaye's band on Friday nights, and then they returned to kneel in prayer at Holy Mass on Sunday morning. For 40 years, from 1925 to 1978, Irwin's Winnipesaukee Gardens Ballroom was the place to be. Overnight, the Irwin family and volunteers transformed the ballroom into a sanctuary where priests assigned to Our Lady of the Lakes in Lakeport offered Holy Mass during the summer resort season. (Courtesy of Irwin Marine.)

Founded on July 21, 1884, three months after the Diocese of Manchester was established and 10 years before Franklin was incorporated as a city, St. Paul's Parish opened its doors. In 1889, Bishop Bradley administered the sacrament of confirmation and celebrated Holy Mass there. By 1902, the congregation outgrew the original church. Bishop Bradley rededicated the church after its enlargement. (Courtesy of the Ken Francher collection.)

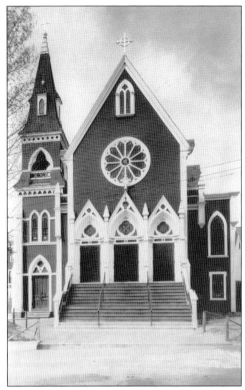

Known as the champion of youth, Rev. Msgr. Richard Boner founded Camp Fatima for boys in 1949 and Camp Bernadette for girls in 1953. Fatima is located on Upper Suncook Lake, the Abenaki name meaning "At the Rocky Place." The Catholic faith is central to recreational camping philosophy and permeates every aspect of daily life. The Church's call is to serve as Christ would. Weekly Mass is celebrated, and many opportunities for prayer and holiness abound at both camps. Campers are seen here diving enthusiastically into chilly, fresh lake waters. (Courtesy of Diocesan Camp Archives.)

Camp Bernadette is on the shore of Lake Wentworth, named for New Hampshire's British colonial governor and the state's seventh largest lake. This diocesan ministry exemplifies traditional overnight camps that teach sportsmanship and provide healthy Catholic activities where young people make lifelong friends and mature in their faith. Camp Bernadette's pinewood chapel engages Catholic youth in the natural presence of God. (Courtesy of Rosemary Sullivan.)

Camp Bernadette, purchased by Rev. Msgr. Richard Boner for less than $50,000 and now valued in excess of $3 million, continues to serve Catholic campers. It is a retreat center and can be reserved for parish events. In this recent photograph, those assisting at Holy Mass partake in the Communion of Christ while standing in the glory of the Father's creation. (Courtesy of Rosemary Sullivan.)

Following the Second Vatican Council, contemporary and folk music were introduced to and accepted in some parish liturgies and social events. Seen here is a Sacred Heart brothers' band entertaining with acoustic and electric guitars and double-bass. Bishop Ernest Primeau is seated with the audience. (Courtesy of St. André Bissette Parish.)

Joseph Oliva Huot was born and raised on the shores of New Hampshire's largest natural lake, Winnipesaukee. His upbringing in Sacred Heart Parish and education at Laconia Public High School prepared him for a life of leadership. Success in business management and volunteer service on the board of education earned him the public's trust. At age 36, he was elected mayor of his native city. He was a delegate to the 1964 Democratic National Convention and elected to the 89th Congress, 1965–1967. In this photograph, he is shown with Pres. Lyndon Baines Johnson signing into law the Medicare Act, which he coauthored. Laconia's technical center at his alma mater is named in his honor. (Courtesy of Dave Huot.)

Irene Huot, an accomplished woman, was a prominent member of Sacred Heart Parish and women's civic groups. She supported her husband's public service and personally influenced local, state, and national politics. She owned and managed a successful dress shop in Laconia. Irene is shown here dancing with Pres. Lyndon Baines Johnson at the Inaugural Ball on January 20, 1965. (Courtesy of Dave Huot.)

Five

MONADNOCK DEANERY

ISOLATED MOUNTAIN

True to its native meaning "Isolated Mountain," Monadnock Deanery's parishes are widespread, which made it difficult for 19th-century Catholics to have access to priests and the sacraments. Catholics experienced a measured welcome in urban areas in the 20th century. A Boy Scout attending Holy Mass at St. Patrick Parish in Jaffrey insisted that he saw a Madonna-like apparition in the brush. "A lady is standing there," he told everyone. In response to his fervent and psychologically examined belief in the presence of Our Lady, this stone grotto was built by Rev. Peter McDonough in the 1940s and remains in her honor. (Courtesy of St. Patrick Parish Archives.)

ST.BERNARD'S CATHOLIC CHURCH
KEENE, NEW HAMPSHIRE

Founded during the American Civil War, St. Bernard Parish was the westernmost Catholic church in New Hampshire. As early as 1844, Catholics living in this extreme, rural forested area of the state found ways to inform each other when missionary priests would arrive to celebrate Holy Mass in family homes and bring the sacraments to all who could gather to receive them. In 1862, Catholics in Keene collected their resources and, with the blessing of Bishop Bacon, erected a church in that city. (Courtesy of the Ken Francher collection.)

Outgrowing the original 1885 wooden church, parishioners of St. Patrick Parish dug up and hauled fieldstones to the church property until there were enough to construct a larger sanctuary. A rural Gothic-style temple was completed in 1917. Stones of all sizes create a broken ashlar, which was erected in an organic pattern, measures 107 feet long and 57 feet wide, and has a 57-foot tower. This early-20th-century photograph records the many parishioners driving automobiles to and assisting at Holy Mass. (Courtesy of St. Patrick Parish Archives.)

Built in 1828, this private residence became Our Lady of Monadnock Academy in 1948. It is located on Main Street, Jaffrey, across from the rectory. The teaching Sisters of Notre Dame and the Sisters of Mercy made it their convent. Protecting their 19th-century family against attacks from indigenous warriors, original residents constructed the home with interior wooden window shutters as shields from incoming arrows. (Author's collection.)

In 1874, Catholics were not permitted to buy land or build churches on Main Street in Peterborough. Wealth among the earliest Irish immigrants was rare, but Hubert-Brennan Murphy purchased a scenic hilltop and assisted in building St. Peter Catholic Church there. Secular rancor erupted with complaints from Protestants that the church and cemetery spoiled the view. (Courtesy of the of Msgr. Charles DesRuisseaux collection.)

Divine Mercy Parish invited members of St. Peter's Parish in Peterborough to join its 21st-century family after more than 120 years of sustaining a historic church in need of prohibitively expensive repair. Confirming that religious life continues under a different roof, Rev. Msgr. Gerald Belanger and the parish council preserved and showcase this ancient icon of the Madonna and Child in the welcoming church. (Courtesy of Divine Mercy Parish.)

As St. Denis Parish in Harrisville declined in membership and was no longer able to financially sustain the physical structures, the congregation merged with two additional parishes in a newly constructed, larger and more amenable edifice. Demonstrating that religious life continues, Divine Mercy Parish preserved and prominently features the crucifix reverenced by Harrisville Catholics for 116 years. (Courtesy of Divine Mercy Parish.)

Divine Mercy Parish was established to bring three congregations, including St. Patrick in Bennington, together as a united church. Parish leadership exemplifies the healing ministry of transformation by incorporating artifacts from each church. Seen here, the reredos that adorned St. Patrick Parish, Bennington, for more than a century now draws the faithful to the source and summit of a modern church, where the historic high altar looks like it has been here forever. (Courtesy of Divine Mercy Parish.)

In 1937, Episcopalians Sibyl and Douglas Sloane purchased property in Rindge. The Hurricane of 1938 destroyed hundreds of trees, revealing a clear view of the Grand Monadnock Mountain. In 1944, their son, Army Air Corps pilot Sanderson "Sandy" Sloane, perished in Germany. The Sloanes built an open-air sanctuary for Sandy's memorial service. This exquisite space became the Cathedral of the Pines, where people of all faiths come to worship. Congregants of St. Peter's in Peterborough celebrated Labor Day on their 75th anniversary at this hilltop cathedral. This photograph of the 1965 ecumenical service held at the Cathedral of the Pines includes Catholic, Hindu, Jewish, Native American, and Protestant leaders from the world over. (Courtesy of Patricia J. Vargas, executive director of Cathedral of the Pines.)

New Hampshire Knights of Columbus, founded in 1899, maintain a highly visible presence throughout their statewide councils. Known and respected for their acts of patriotism and devout faith, the Knights were welcomed by the citizens of Keene as they marched in the 1950 Memorial Day parade. (Courtesy of New Hampshire Knights of Columbus.)

Six

ROCKINGHAM DEANERY
MARQUESS, PRIME MINISTER, LEADER OF THE HOUSE OF LORDS

Dated from a convent of nuns dedicated to Our Lady of Mercy at Seville, Spain, in 1568, this authoritative figure of the Blessed Virgin Mary was adopted by Irish and American Sisters of Mercy. Stationed at the 19th-century Mercy sisters' missions in Maine and New Hampshire, Our Lady of Mercy occupies a prominent place in Windham's Warde Health Center. (Author's collection.)

St. Thomas Aquinas Church and Rectory, West Derry, N.H.

Manchester's neighboring town of Derry listed five or six Catholic families in 1868. As a mission of St. Anne's in Manchester, Rev. William McDonald celebrated Holy Mass in private homes and public buildings. In 1888, a formal parish, featured in this postcard, was dedicated to St. Thomas Aquinas. For 50 years, this parish could not call the faithful to the *Angelus*, Holy Mass, weddings, or funerals until Rev. John Redden donated bronze bells. The first resident pastor ministered to Catholics living in Derry, Epping, Goff's Falls, Salem, Windham, Chester, and Sandown, frequently traveling a circuit of approximately 40 miles. (Courtesy of the Ken Francher collection.)

John Leddy Jr. made a name for himself in Epping that still endures. He purchased farmland and built the first grain elevator in the area with a capacity of 7,000 bushels. He built Leddy block, which consisted of businesses housed in buildings of brick, iron, and granite. He was a civic leader. Determined to establish a parish in Epping, a mission of Exeter, the Leddy, Roy, Thayer, and Kenny families secured the Roy house for celebration of the first Holy Mass. The Roy house is still occupied and located less than 100 yards from the former St. Joseph, Epping's first Catholic church, dedicated in 1898. (Courtesy of the Epping Historical Society.)

84

In 1900, there were 12 to 15 Catholics living in Pelham. They planned a whole Sunday of travel over rough roads in carriages to assist at Holy Mass in Salem or in Massachusetts. Between 1902 and 1905, electric railway came to Hudson, Pelham, and Salem, resulting in an influx of Catholics. Until 1913, Holy Mass was celebrated in the Pelham Town Hall. On May 29, 1910, Pelham became a mission of St. Joseph Parish in Salem. In 1913, Rev. John McNamara acquired land to construct a small church. St. Patrick's Church, captured in this postcard, was dedicated by Bishop Guertin on September 24, 1913. (Courtesy of the Ken Francher collection.)

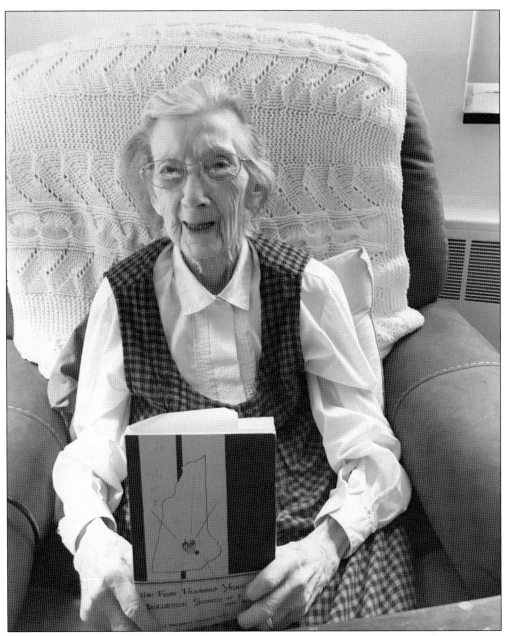

Sr. Mary Benigna, RSM, a highly accomplished woman religious, happily anticipates her upcoming 103rd birthday as the oldest Sister of Mercy in New Hampshire. Orphaned as a young girl, she was separated from her siblings. The Kavanaugh family brought her to the Mercy convent, where she was formally educated. She made her first profession at age 15. Insisting that they be educated before becoming educators, she and the sisters were taught by Saint Anselm's Benedictine monks in Our Lady of Grace Private Academy. There, she earned her bachelor's degree in Latin and taught herself Greek. In addition to a lifetime teaching career, she became editor of the *Magnificat* magazine and was the first sister in New Hampshire to complete her master's degree at Catholic University of America. Sister Benigna is the author of the book *The First Hundred Years*, written for the centennial anniversary of the Sisters of Mercy. (Courtesy of the Sisters of Mercy.)

Seven

Seacoast Deanery

Isles to Inlands,
First Permanent Settlements

Our Lady manifested the medal to St. Catherine Labouré on November 27, 1830, in the motherhouse of the Daughters of Charity of St. Vincent de Paul and St. Louise de Marillac, in Paris. Catherine saw Our Lady standing on a globe, with rays of light streaming from her outstretched hands. Framing the figure was the following inscription: "O Mary, conceived without sin, pray for us who have recourse to thee." With approval of the Catholic Church, the first medals were made and distributed in 1832. (Courtesy of the Central Association of the Miraculous Medal.)

Established in 1851, St. Mary was the first Catholic parish in Portsmouth. The humble structure was destroyed by a suspicious fire in 1871. Within three years, it was replaced with a brick edifice, named Church of the Immaculate Conception and dedicated by Portland's Bishop James Augustine Healy. For 155 years, parishioners and visitors to this exceptionally beautiful sanctuary have been welcomed by angelic guardians, Christ crucified, and saints. (All, author's collection.)

Desiring to celebrate Holy Mass when and where possible, seacoast Catholics made their way in the early 1900s to the Hampton Casino, where the ballroom was transformed into a sanctuary during winter months. In the spring of 1917, St. Patrick, a mission of St. Joseph Cathedral, was dedicated and available exclusively in summer months. (Courtesy of Hampton Historical Society.)

Plans for a more modern church began in 1945 and came to fruition three years later. Our Lady of the Miraculous Medal was prepared in time for the first Midnight Mass to be celebrated in 310 years of Hampton history on December 25, 1948. (Courtesy of a Hampton merchant.)

Wilhelmina Elders Wiegman and her husband, Joseph Wiegman, MD, devout Catholics, sheltered a family of German Jews in their home during World War II's terrible final 10 months. The family diary recounts, "After completing her studies, Wil worked among Holland's poorest as a social worker. Jos completed his medical training and naval service." Wil and Jos married in 1957 in Holland and were able to immigrate to the United States with help from Catholic Emigration Counsel by July 1959. After completing his medical residency in Worcester, the family moved to Somersworth in 1961. There, Jos opened a practice as a family doctor. The family belonged to the Holy Trinity Parish for five decades. (Courtesy of Leo Wiegman.)

Born and baptized on May 16, 1905, in Dover, William Gagnon was inclined early in his youth to take care of others. Discerning this vocation, he was inspired by and accepted into the Hospitaller Order of St. John of God, founded in the late 1530s in Granada, Spain. Brother William professed his vows on November 20, 1932, dedicating his life to caring for the sick, injured, and misplaced. His missionary work brought him to the Bui-Chu Mission in North Vietnam. There, he and his brothers ministered to thousands of refugees. After 17 years of apostolic works, he died in 1972 and is buried among the Vietnamese people. On December 14, 2016, Pope Francis declared him venerable, recognizing that Brother Gagnon lived the three theological and four cardinal virtues to a heroic degree. (Courtesy of Dover Historical Society.)

This dedication on Memorial Day in 1957 of the Marine Memorial, located at Hampton Beach, is the result of a Catholic layman's love and perseverance. The son of William E. Downs, US Army captain William D. Downs died on his return to the United States after having served with Adm. William Halsey and Gen. Douglas MacArthur in World War II. Downs Sr. dedicated seven years of his life as chair and member of the New Hampshire Memorial Committee. These volunteers raised funds, designed the statue, and secured all the permissions needed to place a mourning mother as a permanent monument recording the names of 258 veterans. Dedicated to those lost at sea, this memorial, a first in the nation, ushered legislation that enabled every state to erect similar memorials. (Courtesy of Hampton Historical Society.)

In the 1960s, the Wentworth Hotel, a resort in New Castle, was a mission station of Immaculate Conception Church in Portsmouth. As the youngest of three priests, Rev. Charles DesRuisseaux met altar boys at the Wentworth on Sunday mornings between Mother's Day and Columbus Day to celebrate Holy Mass. Altar boys competed with each other to serve Holy Mass at the Wentworth, where they were treated to breakfast. They loved the popovers. Latin Mass held in the ballroom, was celebrated *ad orientem*, facing east. While in Portsmouth, Fr. Charles DesRuisseaux faced the people in accordance with Vatican Council II decrees. Catholics assisting at Holy Mass in the Wentworth were among the first in America to participate in postconciliar liturgy. (Courtesy of New Castle Historical Society.)

Eight

SOUGHEAN DEANERY
WAITING AND WATCHING PLACE

In the Constitution Ineffabilis Deus, approved December 8, 1854, Pope Pius IX pronounced and defined that the Blessed Virgin Mary "in the first instance of her conception, by a singular privilege and grace granted by God, in view of the merits of Jesus Christ, the Saviour of the human race, was preserved exempt from all stain of original sin." Mary's garden in Nashua provides a place to wait and watch under the protection of the Blessed Virgin. (Courtesy of Immaculate Conception Parish.)

Four of the six women registered in the first nurse training class at St. Joseph Hospital graduated. The photographer posing these 1910 professional nurses chose a close-up portrait, clearly showing the graduates capped and pinned with their fashionable new coiffures. (Courtesy of St. Joseph Hospital Archives.)

1st row: Mary Snow, Isabel Kyle, Alice Gaffney,
2nd row: Elizabeth Haugh

Nurses in training at St. Joseph Hospital lived on campus in quarters adjacent to the sisters' convent. While extending from the hospital, the convent and nurses' residence furnished privacy for prayer and study. A screened-in porch and open terraces allowed fresh air to flow up the hillside. (Courtesy of St. Joseph Hospital Archives.)

Suffering through a life of loss and misery, Marie-Marguerite d'Youville and three women consecrated themselves to God, promising to care for the poor. Marie-Marguerite, known as the mother of universal charity, founded the Sisters of Charity of Montreal and became Canada's first native-born saint in 1871. Her sisters live out the intention of her saintly life. (Author's collection.)

St. Joseph staff was dedicated to the spiritual welfare of patients and their families as well as to their physical care. The hospital chapel reflects both the early-20th-century basic furnishings for communicants and the Gothic elegance of the reredos. Note the absence of kneeler pads and placement of individual chairs rather than pews. Surrounded by sacred images, visitors prayed for God to guide the hands of those caring for loved ones. (Courtesy of St. Joseph Hospital Archives.)

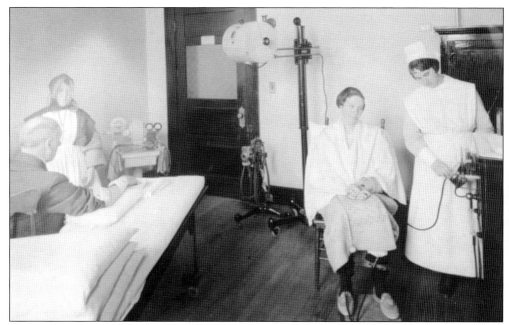

Originally, the hospital was a 78-bed facility, completely equipped with an operating room and chemical, bacteriological, and X-ray laboratories. By 1921, thirty-nine beds were added, and St. Joseph became the first hospital in the state rated a Class A health-care facility by the College of Surgeons. These photographs testify to the genuine and professional care provided to patients. (Both, courtesy of St. Joseph Hospital Archives.)

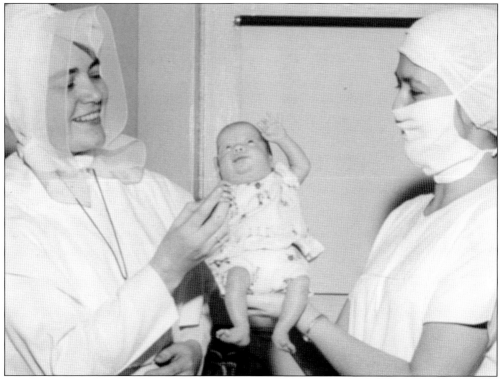

Rivier College was founded in 1933 by the Sisters of the Presentation of Mary in Hudson. The college honors the Sisters of the Presentation of Mary's foundress, Blessed Anne-Marie Rivier, born on December 19, 1768, in Montpezat-sous-Bauzon, France. Crippled from infancy, Anne-Marie was drawn to religious life, but ill health prevented her acceptance to the Sisters of Notre Dame. Dedicated to education, she founded a school in her hometown. Enduring suppression of religious practice during the French Revolution, she founded a new congregation of women religious who educated the most neglected children of France. Sister Antoinette, seated second from the left in the first row, entered the Sisters of the Presentation making her final profession of vows in 1948. She earned her bachelor's and master's degrees in music and education at Rivier College and completed graduate studies in Rhode Island College and the University of Massachusetts at Lowell. Sister Antoinette taught in Berlin; officiated as superior in Dover, Keene, Manchester, and Coventry, Rhode Island; and organized a summer camp for children. She lived 88 years. (Courtesy of Gerald Durette.)

After graduating from Nashua High School and attending Saint Anselm College, Paul Boire earned his pilot's license through the Civil Aeronautics Administration program. He enlisted in the Navy and served on the aircraft carrier USS *Essex*. Ensign Boire was lost at sea off the coast of Trinidad on March 23, 1943. Boire was 22 years old and the first Nashua pilot to lose his life in World War II. In 1945, Nashua Municipal Airfield was officially renamed in his honor. Rev. Amie Boire, his uncle, read the family response and blessed the marker at the dedication ceremony. (Author's collection.)

Born in Nashua, Anita Paul was raised on a farm in Hudson. While playing outside their barn, she saw a plane overhead. Dreams of flying occupied her four-year-old sense of adventure. The daughter of a World War I veteran, Anita exercised her patriotism by working for the War Department in Washington, DC. The attack on Pearl Harbor motivated Anita to enlist in the US Army Air Forces Women Airforce Service Pilots (WASP). She earned her pilot's license and flew stateside missions until 1944. Anita reported that of all the supplies and equipment she transported to the troops, the most precious cargo she ever carried was the Blessed Sacrament. WASP Anita Paul is standing third from left with her copilots. (Courtesy of Texas Women's University Archives.)

Within months of the cessation of World War II, Anita Paul entered the Discalced Carmelite Monastery and took the religious name of Sister Theresa. Although a cloistered nun, during her nearly 65 years as a woman religious, Sister Theresa flew as a passenger to Japan, South Korea, and Kenya, establishing Carmelite monasteries for her international sisters. Sister Theresa Paul is shown here in her later years as a Discalced Carmelite nun. (Courtesy of the Carmelite Monastery Archives.)

Dr. Mary A. Sweeney, member of St. Patrick Parish, Nashua, earned her medical license from Tufts College Medical School, graduating cum laude. Dr. Sweeney lived a frugal life as a devout single laywoman. She practiced medicine at St. Joseph Hospital. In 1972, she bequeathed a gift to her parish that funded renovation of the convent into 31 affordable, safe apartments for women with limited financial resources. (Courtesy of the Mary Sweeney Apartment Center.)

Massachusetts senator John Fitzgerald Kennedy chose Nashua, New Hampshire, to announce his candidacy for president. This first-in-the-nation political event led to the successful election of Kennedy as the 35th president of the United States. As evidenced in this photograph, Senator Kennedy was welcomed in Nashua with hopeful support. (Courtesy of the New Institute of Politics, Saint Anselm College.)

Nine

UPPER VALLEY DEANERY
BESIDE THE LONG, TIDAL RIVER

In 1930, Joseph Bourgeau of Blodgett's Landing bought land on Main Street in New London and built the structure that became the first Our Lady of Fatima Church in the diocese. The front of the building functioned as an ice cream and candy store, while the backroom was used for Holy Mass. Priests from LaSalette Seminary in Enfield officiated. In 1936, Our Lady of Fatima was established as a mission church of St. Helena in Enfield. (Courtesy of Our Lady of Fatima Guild.)

Virgil Barber was born into an Episcopalian family in Claremont. Inspired by the life of St. Francis Xavier, the Barber family converted to Catholicism. He and his wife terminated their marital status. Their children entered Catholic boarding schools. Virgil was ordained to the priesthood on December 3, 1822, by Bishop Jean Lefebvre de Cheverus, who directed him to return to Claremont. There, he built a church and academy recorded as the first Catholic institutes in New Hampshire. Within a few years, the academy closed, and Barber was removed from ministry. He abandoned the estimated 100 members of St. Mary Parish to be a missionary among the native tribes of Maine and Vermont. Old St. Mary's is the second oldest Catholic structure standing in New England. (Courtesy of the Richard Tetreault collection.)

The Sisters of the Holy Names of Jesus and Mary is a religious congregation of women founded in Québec by the Blessed Eulalie Durocher (Mother Marie-Rose) to educate young girls. They were the second community of professed sisters to establish a convent in New Hampshire. Between 1880 and 1895, they administered St. Mary's School in Claremont. Before the Sisters of Mercy arrived in 1896, a laywoman kept the school open and operating. (Author's collection.)

A Claremont priest, Rev. Maurice Sekiewicz, gained considerable attention as administrator of St. Joseph's Polish parish between 1924 and 1936. To alleviate pervasive poverty, he gained the bishop's permission to introduce parish festivals. The bishop was unaware that the festivals included secular entertainment of the Roaring Twenties. As the threat of war became a reality, Reverend Sekiewicz externed from the diocese to Poland, where he joined the army as a chaplain. He was captured and killed as a prisoner of war. (Courtesy of Upper Valley Antiques.)

Bishop John B. Delany's epitaph reads, "His reign was short but rich in promise." He was wise. Realizing that Catholics needed to broaden their understanding of faith beyond the ledges and wetlands of New Hampshire, he served as editor of the *Guidon*, the first Diocesan publication. He was resolute. A decision made was an action implemented! Bishop Delany died of acute appendicitis on June 11, 1906. In his brief episcopacy (1904–1906), he dedicated two parishes in the diocese: St. Catherine of Siena in Charlestown, located on the southwest state border along the Connecticut River, and Our lady of the Lake in Lakeport, between Paugus and Opechee Bays. (Courtesy of St. Jean Baptist Parish Archives.)

Holy Mass was first celebrated in Lebanon in 1835, nearly three quarters of a century after its founding. About 15 Catholic families immigrated to the city, located along the Connecticut River and Mascoma Lake, which powered a successful mill district. Mascoma is named for the chief of the Squakheag Indians. French and Irish secured employment in furniture mills, a tannery, and clothing factories and with the Boston Railroad. By 1876, Bishop Healy of Portland established Sacred Heart Parish, consecrated in 1879. The first school was staffed by lay teachers who educated students for 11 years. In 1909, the Sisters of Mercy arrived to reopen the school. (Courtesy of a private collector.)

John Breen, from Tipperary, Ireland, came to America in 1847. He built an imposing summer home on the north end of Great Island in Lake Sunapee. There, he erected a tent on his island property and made arrangements with Rev. James J. Hogan to offer Holy Mass. Every Sunday morning, the *Lady Woodsum* steamer cruised around the lake, picking up churchgoers for Holy Mass on the island. Enthusiasm grew, and soon, Breen donated land and $100 to build a church. A total of $17,000 was raised. Before the church was built, the benefactor fell ill and died. Legend tells that a person who played an important part in the fundraising absconded with all the money. Our Lady of the Lake was never built. (Courtesy of Sunapee Historical Society.)

Claimed as the "Chosen Vale" in the late 18th century, religious zeal thrived in Mascoma Valley until Shaker membership diminished, and the property, in excess of 1,000 acres, was closed. La Salette fathers, founded in 1846 after the apparition of the Blessed Virgin Mary to two young children in the French Alps, opened a seminary on the former Shaker grounds where religious life continues. In 1928, the Sisters of St. Martha arrived to attend to the domestic needs of the religious community, much like the Shaker sisters did in the previous century. (Courtesy of the LaSalette Fathers gift shop.)

In her 65 years of life, Mary A. Keane, a consecrated laywoman, inclined her exceptional intellectual capacity towards teaching and used her inherited wealth towards caring for the poor. In 1915, with permission of her spiritual director, Mary retired to Enfield. Beside the waters of Lake Mascoma, which she called the "Antechamber to Heaven," she built a seminary dormitory, infirmary, retreat house, and chapel, dedicated to the Sacred Heart of Jesus. Mary is the only woman buried among the La Salette missionaries in their cemetery. As benefactress to the church, Mary returned all the spiritual and worldly gifts bestowed on her from her benefactor, God alone. (Author's collection.)

Ten

WHITE MOUNTAIN DEANERY

CRYSTAL SNOWCAPS
ABOVE THE CLOUDS

The grand approach to what is now known as the Presidential Range was originally named *Apikwahki*, meaning "Land of the Hollows," by the Abenaki. Centered above the main altar in Our Lady of the Mountains Parish, North Conway, the Blessed Virgin Mary is crowned in glory. This oil painting presents the Infant Jesus with open arms, welcoming all. Standing among springtime wildflowers before a verdant field leading to the foothills and eventually to snow-covered Mount Washington, rising 6,288 feet above sea level, one is reminded that Mary is the spiritual mother in all seasons. (Courtesy of Our Lady of the Mountains Parish Archives.)

The Blessed Virgin Mary's title "Our Lady of the Snows" began in AD 352 with the prayers of a Roman couple. Mary appeared in a vision to both the husband and Pope Liberius with instructions to build a church in her honor. Our Lady sent a midsummer snowfall defining the floor plan on Esquiline Hill in Rome, now Basilica Sanctae Mariae Maioris. The fifth bishop of Manchester purchased a former Baptist church and relocated it as Our Lady of the Snows Mission in Franconia. Religious life continues there today. (Courtesy of the Catholic Art Association.)

In October 1871, the Drexel family of Philadelphia visited the White Mountains. The family hiked Tuckerman's Ravine and observed artists at work in Franconia Notch. In her lifetime, Katharine founded the Sisters of the Blessed Sacrament for Indians and Negroes and built schools and churches for the most neglected children in America. The Reverend Mother Katharine Drexel, SBS, was canonized in 2000. (Courtesy of Cumberland County Historical Society.)

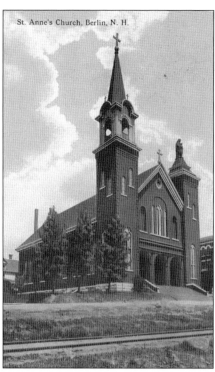

St. Anne's Parish in Berlin was formed in 1867. The original church was completed in November 1881. By 1900, the predominantly French population outgrew the original church. The brick Roman-Gothic church is often referred to as the Cathedral of the North Country in recognition of its size and inspired beauty. (Courtesy of the Ken Francher collection.)

On September 15, 1889, St. Regis Academy opened to 400 students in a former hotel known as the Cascade House. In 1911, the building was demolished and replaced with a beautiful brick structure. Berlin is the source of several vocations. Many priests attribute this blessing to the Sisters of the Presentation of Mary, who taught at the academy and who continuously asked young girls and boys if they were considering becoming a sister or a priest. (Courtesy of the Ken Francher collection.)

St. Rose of Lima is the patron for all South America. She was drawn to a life of strict, oftentimes severe, religious practices. Although she remained a virgin and a recluse, she was skilled in needlework and sold lace and embroidery to help her family and the poor. She was canonized by Pope Clement X on April 12, 1671. This photograph shows the original church in Littleton. (Courtesy of St. Rose of Lima Parish Archives.)

When the parish outgrew the original wooden church, built in 1882, the decision was made to construct a permanent edifice. Parishioners and workmen shown here are lifting a steel beam during construction of the new St. Rose of Lima Church, made of fieldstones. Visitors to St. Rose of Lima Church and Rectory, located on Clay and High Streets, are reminded that they are indeed between heaven and earth! (Courtesy of St. Rose of Lima Parish Archives.)

Known affectionately as the woman in the mirror, Josephine Corey is seen here looking over her shoulder through the organ mirror and playing liturgical music for Holy Mass. Josephine carried on her music ministry with St. Rose of Lima Parish for 70 years. (Courtesy of St. Rose of Lima Parish Archives.)

This photograph shows altar servers on the new altar of St. Rose of Lima. Prior to the Second Vatican Council, this ministry was reserved exclusively for boys and young men. (Courtesy of St. Rose of Lima Parish Archives.)

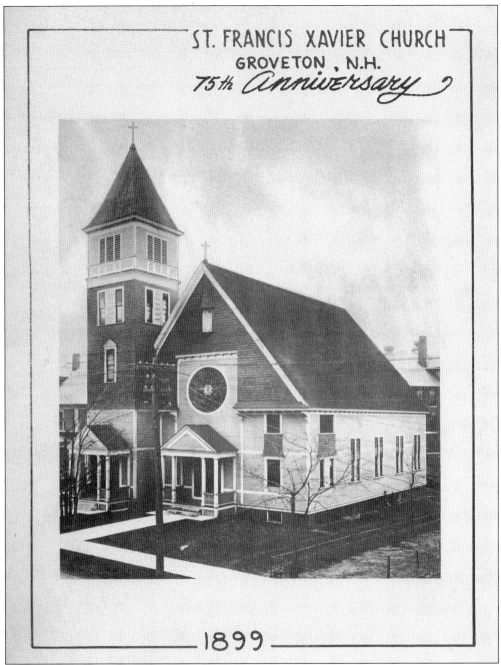

ST. FRANCIS XAVIER CHURCH
GROVETON, N.H.
75th Anniversary

1899

Founded in 1899 in Groveton, Coos County, St. Francis Parish was named for St. Francis Xavier, who was among the first three ordained Jesuits. He labored as a missionary to the East Indies and Asia in the 16th century. The mission came under the pastoral care of Rev. Isidore H. Noiseux, charged with managing all missions and parishes in the Connecticut River valley and in the White Mountain region. (Courtesy of the Msgr. Charles DesRuisseaux collection.)

St. Louis' Hospital, Berlin, N. H.

2489

Berlin's first health-care facility, the Hospital St. Louis, opened in 1905 under the direction of the Sisters of Charity with rooms for 15 patients. It was named for Rev. Louis M. LaPlante, pastor of St. Anne's Parish, who realized the need for professional health-care since his arrival in 1899. (Courtesy of the Ken Francher collection.)

Rev. Louis Ramsay was born in Berlin, studied at Sherbrooke Seminary, and was ordained in 1916. He enlisted in the US Army Chaplain Corps and served in France with the 301st Engineers and at Camp Devens. Father Ramsay served as pastor of three French parishes, including St. Theresa in Manchester. St. Theresa School was renovated into senior housing with an additional apartment center built for seniors and individuals with handicaps that was named in honor of Father Ramsay. (Courtesy of Eastpoint Properties.)

The Durette family is seen here after the wedding of Amira Nocet and Laurier Durette at St. Matthew Church in Whitefield. Rev. Napoleon Durette is the uncle of the bride. (Courtesy of Gerald Durette.)

Lucien Gosselin was born in Whitefield. His family moved to Manchester, where Bishop Guertin encouraged his aptitude for art. After graduating from the Académie Julian in Paris, Gosselin returned in 1916 to teach at the Manchester Institute of Arts and Sciences. World War I affected him so profoundly that he dedicated himself to creating sacred art and memorials for military veterans. (Courtesy of the Currier Gallery of Arts.)

As a young priest, Pope John Paul II was among thousands of passengers on Canon Mountain's tramway ascending to the summit. During Bishop Leo O'Neil's *ad limina* visit, His Holiness asked him a couple of times, "Where are you from?" "Manchester," he replied. Pope John Paul queried, "New Hampshire?" "Yes, your Holiness, New Hampshire." The Bishop of Rome smiled and said, "Canon Mountain." The surprised prelate questioned, "May I ask how you know Canon Mountain?" The Supreme Pontiff of the Universal Church, now St. Pope John Paul II, exclaimed, "I skied it!" (Courtesy of Steve O'Connell.)

Holding their skis, the faithful assist at Holy Mass in Our Lady of the Mountains Shrine Church in Bretton Woods. At the opening of every ski season, the local pastor blesses the skis and those who will experience the adventure of alpine and cross-country skiing, invigorating the mind, body, and soul. (Courtesy of the New Hampshire Ski Museum.)

Hannes Schneider (second from left), a Catholic world-class skier, was rescued from a concentration camp in Nazi Germany by an international financier who lived in North Conway. Harvey Gibson used his German holdings to negotiate with Heinrich Luitpold Himmler to release Schneider and transport him to America. Hannes Schneider developed the Alberg technique of skiing. He taught Rev. Alfred Daniszewski how to ski! (Courtesy of North Conway Public Library.)

In 1922, Arnold Lunn (seated to the right, next to Hannes Schneider) introduced paired poles through which the skier must pass, creating the modern Alpine slalom race. Lunn converted to Catholicism and was a member of Our Lady of the Mountains Parish. He became a prolific writer, publishing books on skiing, mountaineering, philosophy, and Christianity. (Courtesy of North Conway Public Library.)

Sr. Hermeniguilde LaBante, a Daughter of the Charity of the Sacred Heart of Jesus, devoted her ministry to Christian unity. During her professed life in Littleton, New Hampshire, and France, Sister LaBante wrote to an estimated 5,000 sisters in a dozen countries requesting their prayers for unity and mailing addresses of Anglican, Protestant, and Eastern Rite women religious. From adolescence, she was consumed with the "agony of separation" of Christian women religious from the Catholic Church. In one of her thousands of missives, she wrote, "Since 1953, I have had the privilege and grace of having very fraternal relationships with our dear Sisters who are separated from us yet are so very fervent, so very desiring unity." In addition to her devotion to unity, she became an accomplished musician and sought-after teacher. Sister LaBante is the first sister on the left in the first row. (Courtesy of the Daughters of the Charity of the Sacred Heart of Jesus Archives.)

LAKE GLORIETTE AND THE BALSAMS—DIXVILLE NOTCH, N. H.

During the summer months of 1954, Holy Mass was offered in the theater of the Balsams Resort Hotel in Dixville Notch. The consecrated chapel was dedicated to Archbishop Saint William of York, canonized in 1227 by Pope Honorius. Priests responsible for the mission station traveled 11 miles from Errol, the same distance from Colebrook, and 23 miles from North Stratford on rarely reliable roads. The chapel was deconsecrated when access to neighboring churches became less burdensome for summer vacationers. (Courtesy of the Ken Francher collection.)

In 1943, the Balsams almost became a Jesuit seminary. The US Army needed a large property to use as a hospital for wounded veterans returning from war. Medical Corps officers designated the Jesuit monastery in Weston, Massachusetts, as the "sought-out" location for 1,600 patients and a staff of 185. Searching for a place to relocate, the Balsams was chosen, and the Jesuits made an offer. Ultimately, the Army did not take Weston, and the religious community did not have to evacuate. They forfeited funds used for the down payment on the hotel and were fined legal fees. (Courtesy of the Ken Francher collection.)

124

Nestled between Franconia and Crawford Notches, which rise to the south of Twin Mountain, St. Patrick Church, named for Ireland's patron saint in 1915, welcomed many Irish immigrants. The church is built of stones from the nearby Ammonoosuc River. The river was named by the Abenaki to describe "a small, narrow fishing place." (Courtesy of the Ken Francher collection.)

This 1884 chart demonstrates the disparate locations of pioneer missions and churches existing in the diocese's founding year. With 27 zealous priests, courageous sisters, hardworking laity, and less than 20 houses of worship, Bishop Denis M. Bradley began building the city of God in the new diocese. (Courtesy of the Manchester Diocesan Archives.)

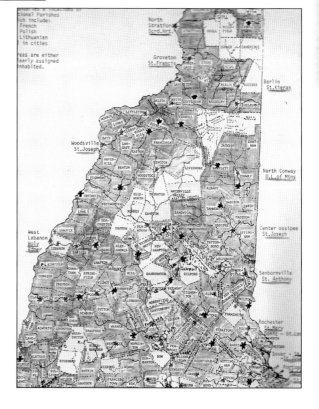

This 1991 chart demonstrates the steady, statewide establishment of missions, chapels, churches, schools, and hospitals in the 97-year-old diocese. Steadfast in faith, the Diocese of Manchester trusts in God's mercy as the church prevails. (Courtesy of the Manchester Diocesan Archives.)

Joseph "Salt of the Earth" Fobes, resident of Sugar Hill in Franconia, is seen here with Bishop Emeritus John McCormack. He was known locally as Farmer Fobes, owner and manager of the largest cattle farm in New Hampshire. In his lifetime, Joseph Fobes, a man of integrity, was a husband, father, civic leader, Air Force veteran, Harvard graduate, convert to Catholicism, teacher, and real estate agent for the diocese. In every manner of his life, Joseph was a gift to the church and gave freely of his time, his resources, and his heart in return for his boundless faith in God. (Courtesy of the Manchester Diocesan Archives.)

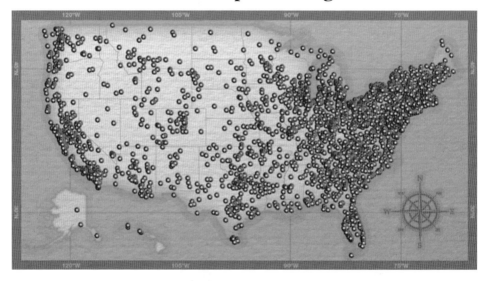